Heaven

DISCOVERY SERIES BIBLE STUDY
For individuals or groups

According to a bestselling book, heaven is for real. But it's not a book written by a midwestern US pastor about his son that solidifies this truth for us. What tells us the unshakable reality of heaven is a book that was completed a couple of thousand years ago. The Bible spells out for us in no uncertain terms that there is a place of God's presence that we all should aspire to. It is God's abode, and it is because He is there that we should want to go there as well. In this booklet by Richard W. DeHaan, who was president of this ministry for many years, we see heaven for what the Bible says it is—a place of hope, blessing, and encouragement for all who embrace God's Son Jesus Christ as Savior. May you find peace and comfort from this study of the home our God is preparing for us.

—*Dave Branon*
Discovery House Publishers

This Discovery Series Bible Study is based on
Our Eternal Home (RD911), one of the popular Discovery Series booklets from this
ministry. Find out more about Discovery Series at
discoveryseries.org

Requests for permission to quote from this book should be directed to:
Permissions Department, Discovery House Publishers, PO Box 3566, Grand Rapids, MI 49501,
or contact us by e-mail at permissionsdept@dhp.org

DISCOVERY HOUSE

P U B L I S H E R S®

Managing Editor: Dave Branon
Study Guide questions: Dave Branon
Graphic Design: Steve Gier

COVER PHOTO:
Adam Jackson via FreeImages.com

INSIDE PHOTOS:
thejobathome via MorgueFile.com, p.6; DTL via MorgueFile.com, p.14; Ladyheart via MorgueFile.com, p.16;
cs3designs via MorgueFile.com, p.17; o0o0xmods0o0o via MorgueFile.com, p.23; Dirk Vermeylen via Pixabay.com, p.28;
SRCHEN via MorgueFile.com, p.29; bullboy via MorgueFile.com, p.38; clarita via MorgueFile.com, p.40; PhotoDisc, p.41;
cristinasz via MorgueFile.com, p.50; Holger Foerstemann via MorgueFile.com, p.52; Maeva Bac via FreeImages.com, p.53;
© Barbara Bosworth / www.heirlooms-gallery.com, p.55; Brady Smith via FreeImages.com, p. 58; Seemann via
MorgueFile.com, kolobsek via MorgueFile.com, and Johnny Maroun via FreeImages.com, p.60

ISBN: 978-1-62707-064-5
Printed in the United States of America
First Printing in 2014

Table of Contents

How To Use
DISCOVERY SERIES BIBLE STUDIES

The Purpose

The Discovery Series Bible Study (DSBS) series provides assistance to pastors and lay leaders in guiding and teaching fellow Christians with lessons adapted from RBC Ministries Discovery Series booklets and supplemented with items taken from the pages of *Our Daily Bread*. The DSBS series uses the inductive study method to help Christians understand the Bible more clearly.

The Format

READ: Each DSBS book is divided into a series of lessons. For each lesson, you will read a few pages that will give you insight into one aspect of the overall study. Included in some studies will be FOCAL POINT and TIME OUT FOR THEOLOGY segments to help you think through the material. These can be used as discussion starters for group sessions.

RESPOND: At the end of the reading is a two-page STUDY GUIDE to help participants respond to and reflect on the subject. If you are the leader of a group study, ask each member to preview the STUDY GUIDE before the group gets together. Don't feel that you have to work your way through each question in the STUDY GUIDE; let the interest level of the participants dictate the flow of the discussion. The questions are designed for either group or individual study. Here are the parts of that guide:

MEMORY VERSE: A short Scripture passage that focuses your thinking on the biblical truth at hand and can be used for memorization. You might suggest memorization as a part of each meeting.

WARMING UP: A general interest question that can foster discussion (group) or contemplation (individual).

THINKING THROUGH: Questions that will help a group or a student interact with the reading. These questions help drive home the critical concepts of the book.

DIGGING IN: An inductive study of a related passage of Scripture, reminding the group or the student of the importance of Scripture as the final authority.

GOING FURTHER: A two-part wrap-up of the response: REFER suggests ways to compare the ideas of the lesson with teachings in other parts of the Bible. REFLECT challenges the group or the learner to apply the teaching in real life.

OUR DAILY BREAD: After each STUDY GUIDE session will be an *Our Daily Bread* article that relates to the topic. You can use this for further reflection or for an introduction to a time of prayer.

Go to the Leader's and User's Guide on page 61 for further suggestions about using this Discovery Series Bible Study.

1

God's Dwelling Place and Ours

The mention of the word *heaven* raises at once a number of questions. Is there really such a place? If so, where is it? What is heaven like? Will everyone go there, or just a certain privileged few? And then, some will ask, "Do we go there immediately at death, or does the soul 'sleep' for a while?"

For many people in the early decades of the twenty-first century, these questions are not relevant. They scoff at the idea of life after death, and they ridicule the belief in a heaven of eternal bliss and a hell of everlasting punishment. They are convinced that the existence of humans ends at the grave.

Christians do believe in a beautiful place called heaven, and they look forward to eternal life within its gates. Based on their faith in Christ and their trust in God's Word, they anticipate the joys that await them in their eternal home. They look forward to a place where their hopes will be realized, blessings will be given through God's gracious hand, and encouragement to last an eternity awaits. This comforting thought brings healing to the wounds of their earthly existence, and it calms their sorrows.

> The word **heaven** in its singular and plural forms occurs more than six hundred times in Scripture.

The place to find out about heaven is the Bible. The word *heaven* in its singular and plural forms occurs more than six hundred times in Scripture. We are given much information about our eternal home, and in this lesson we will consider it carefully in two aspects: 1. the habitation of God, and 2. the home of departed believers in Jesus Christ.

The Habitation of God

The Bible often speaks of heaven as God's "habitation" and explicitly declares that He dwells there.

Thus says the High and Lofty One who inhabits eternity, whose name is Holy: "I will dwell in the high and holy place, with him who has a contrite and humble spirit, to revive the spirit of the humble, and to revive the heart of the contrite ones" *(ISAIAH 57:15)*.

Solomon also recognized heaven as God's home when he prayed:

May You hear the supplication of Your servant and Your people Israel, when they pray toward this place. Hear in heaven Your dwelling place; and when You hear, forgive *(1 KINGS 8:30)*.

This does not mean that God is absent from earth. His presence is everywhere, but His dwelling place is in heaven. He abides there, and from that location He is present throughout all His creation.

The Bible also teaches that heaven is the location of God's throne. The psalmist declared:

The Lord has established His throne in heaven, and His kingdom rules over all (PSALM 103:19).

God is king of the universe He created; the Bible speaks of "His throne," which He occupies in heaven. From there He rules over the affairs of men. Nebuchadnezzar, the mighty king of Babylon, learned of God's sovereign rulership through firsthand experience. He had become self-centered and proud, and the Lord had temporarily chastened him by a period of severe mental illness. When it was all over, he prayed:

Now I, Nebuchadnezzar, praise and extol and honor the King of heaven, all of whose works are truth, and His ways justice. And those who walk in pride He is able to put down (DANIEL 4:37).

God, the Almighty King, rules in majesty over His entire creation. He holds all things together by His mighty power. He may permit evil men and the rulers of darkness to have their day, but He has not lost control of the world—not for one moment! Although the wicked may rebel against His laws and declare themselves masters of their own destiny, God from heaven is still in command.

Psalm 2 describes the empty efforts of the nations to rebel against the Lord God and against His Christ. Those boasters say:

Let us break Their bonds in pieces and cast away Their cords from us (v. 3).

But the psalmist went on to express the folly and madness of seeking to stand up against the Almighty:

He who sits in the heavens shall laugh; the Lord shall hold them in derision. Then He shall speak to them in His wrath, and distress them in His deep displeasure (vv. 4–5).

Yes, God in heaven has only to speak the word, and all His enemies will be destroyed. When the Bible speaks of heaven as God's throne, therefore, it means that this is the center of His administration, the seat of His authority, the place from which He issues His edicts, commands, and sovereign decrees.

The Bible also teaches that God accepts our worship and hears our prayers in heaven. The Lord told Solomon at the finishing of the temple:

If My people who are called by My name will humble themselves, and pray and seek My face, and turn from their wicked ways, then I will hear from heaven, and will forgive their sin and heal their land (2 CHRONICLES 7:14).

King David, the father of Solomon, had also learned that God hears the prayers of His people. David had earnestly sought God's help, and the Lord had granted him victory over the Philistines. In gratitude he wrote:

In my distress I called upon the LORD, and cried out to God; He heard my voice from His temple, and my cry entered His ears (2 SAMUEL 22:7).

God has promised to listen to the prayers of His people. What a blessing that the same is true for Christians today! Whether we want to confess our sins to Him or just to praise Him, He will hear and respond.

In heaven, God not only accepts the worship of His people on earth, but He also receives the adoration of the heavenly hosts who dwell there with Him. In Hebrews 12:22, for example, we are told of an innumerable company of angels who abide in heaven. The Bible portrays them as constantly worshiping and serving God. They are continually going back and forth, from earth to heaven and from heaven to earth, fulfilling the Lord's instructions.

Are not they all ministering spirits sent forth to minister for those who will inherit salvation? (HEBREWS 1:14).

All this activity centers around God's throne. There they receive their orders, and there they return when their mission is accomplished.

Other angelic beings, the cherubim and seraphim, are with God in heaven. Creatures of service and worship, they attend His throne to extol His holiness and to render praise through obedience.

Heaven is the habitation of God. From there He rules over all creation, hears the prayers of His people, and accepts the worship of His earthly subjects and His heavenly attendants.

The Home of Departed Saints

Not only is heaven God's habitation, but it is also the place where His saints will dwell forever. We can rightly call heaven "our eternal home." Death does not end all; the soul lives on. And for the believer, the soul at death immediately enters forever into the presence of God.

Some teach otherwise. They refer to those who die as being "asleep," and by this they mean that their souls cease to exist until some time of future resurrection. But the term *soul sleep*, as used in this manner, is a misnomer—simply because a soul with no existence apart from the body could not be referred to as "sleeping." If it doesn't exist, it is gone! This means that at some future time God would find it necessary to re-create the entire individual. The body would first have to be resurrected; then it would need to be given a new soul. This is contrary to the teaching of God's Word.

Death involves physical and spiritual separation—not annihilation! Physical death occurs when the soul is separated from the body. Spiritual death is the eternal separation of the soul from God. Although the believer in Christ may die physically, having his soul separated from his body, he can never die spiritually. He will never experience the separation of his soul from God.

My believing friend, this should be a special comfort to you. It means that your Christian loved ones who have died are not separated from the Lord and never will be. When they gave their hearts to Christ, they received life everlasting. Jesus said,

He who hears My word and believes in Him who sent Me has everlasting life (JOHN 5:24).

Those who have died in Christ have entered into the presence of God, and even now they abide with Him in heaven. Jesus taught this truth in His words to Martha at the time of the resurrection of Lazarus. When Jesus arrived at Bethany, four days after Lazarus had died, Martha came out to meet Him and complained, "Lord, if You had been here, my brother would not have died" (John 11:21). Then Christ, assuring Martha that her brother would rise again, stated this beautiful, comforting truth:

I am the resurrection and the life. He who believes in Me, though he may die, he shall live. And whoever lives and believes in Me shall never die (vv. 25–26).

We learn two important lessons from these words of Christ. First, even though believers may die physically, as Lazarus did, their bodies will someday be resurrected. Remember, Jesus said, "I am the resurrection and the life." Second, through faith in Christ the child of God possesses eternal life. Therefore, in the deepest sense of the word, he will never die. That's why Jesus could give the glorious promise, "Whoever lives and believes in Me shall never die."

Yes, the body may perish, but the soul of the Christian lives on—never to be separated from God, the source of life. Those who teach that the soul of man ceases to exist at death deny a clear statement from the lips of our Lord himself. Remember that Jesus said, "Whoever lives and believes in Me shall never die."

 In Christ's Presence

When the believer dies, he departs from this life to go immediately into the presence of Christ. At the moment physical life is ended, therefore, the Christian meets Jesus face to face in his eternal home in heaven. The words of the Lord Jesus at Calvary emphasize this truth. As Christ hung on the accursed tree, one of the dying thieves expressed faith in Him, crying out, "Lord, remember me when You come into Your kingdom" (Luke 23:42). The Lord Jesus gave His word that they would meet again, and not way off in the far distant future. He promised, "*Today* you will be *with Me* in Paradise" (v. 43).

The apostle Paul viewed the period between death and resurrection as a time of joy, blessing, and fellowship in the presence of Christ. He told the believers in Philippi:

For to me, to live is Christ, and to die is gain. But if I live on in the flesh, this will mean fruit from my labor; yet what I shall choose I cannot tell. For I am hard pressed between the two, having a desire to depart and be with Christ, which is far better (PHILIPPIANS 1:21–23).

It's plain to see that the apostle fully expected to be with the Lord the very moment he departed from this life. Because of this he could say, "To die is gain" and "to depart and be with Christ . . . is far better."

In 2 Corinthians 5:6–8, he expressed again his sincere conviction that the day he would leave this body, he would join his Savior in heaven:

So we are always confident, knowing that while we are at home in the body we are absent from the Lord. For we walk by faith, not by sight. We are confident, yes, well pleased rather to be absent from the body and to be present with the Lord.

To give proper emphasis to the tenses used in the Greek, this last verse should read, "We are confident, I say, and willing, rather to be once-for-all away from home as far as the body is concerned, and to be once-for-all at home with the Lord."

Paul was not speaking here about the resurrection of the body. That will occur when the trumpet sounds for the rapture of the church. Rather, he spoke of what happens to the soul immediately following death. When a Christian dies, his soul is ushered into Christ's presence in heaven. Death for the believer brings about an immediate, once-for-all change—from being in our body on earth to being with our Lord in our eternal home.

This is the fulfillment of Jesus' prayer in John 17, spoken shortly before His crucifixion.

Father, I desire that they also whom You gave Me may be with Me where I am, that they may behold My glory which You have given

Me; for You loved Me before the foundation of the world (v. 24).

For the believer, this prayer finds fulfillment at death. He enters heaven and begins to experience all the wonderful blessings of being with the Lord.

SUMMARY

In this lesson we have emphasized two important truths. First, heaven is the habitation of God. It's where the Lord rules over all His creation, accepts the worship of His beings, and hears our prayers. Second, heaven is the home of departed saints, where we will abide forever in the presence of our Savior, the Lord Jesus Christ. Although our bodies may be buried in the grave to be resurrected at the rapture of the church, our souls go immediately to be with the Lord.

Not everyone, however, will enjoy the glories of heaven. There is one condition that must be met if you are to enter that eternal home. The only condition is faith in God's Son, the Lord Jesus Christ. He said,

For God so loved the world that He gave His only begotten Son, that whoever believes in Him should not perish but have everlasting life

(JOHN 3:16).

■ Focal Point

In 2 Corinthians 5, Paul has an informative comment on the difference between our current existence and our heavenly one: "Now we know that if the earthly tent we live in is destroyed, we have a building from God, an eternal house in heaven, not built by human hands" (v. 1 NIV).

MEMORY VERSE
2 Corinthians 5:8—

"We are confident, yes, well pleased rather to be absent from the body and to be present with the Lord."

To understand the importance of the truth that God allows us to dwell with Him forever.

Warming Up

When you begin to think about heaven, what comes to mind? Is it more about a place or is it about who you will share heaven with? Explain.

Thinking Through

1. Richard DeHaan says that the Bible mentions heaven six hundred times. Do you feel that with that many mentions of heaven you have a complete understanding of the place where you will spend eternity?

2. Richard DeHaan brings up an interesting point when he says that God's presence in heaven "does not mean that God is absent from earth" (page 7). So how do we differentiate between God's omniscience on earth and His "habitation" in heaven?

3. Discuss how the following statement relates to our existence in heaven: "Although our bodies may be buried in the grave to be resurrected at the rapture of the church, our souls go immediately to be with the Lord" (page 13).

Going Further

Refer

What does each of these verses tell us about God and His activity in heaven?

1 Kings 8:49:

Hebrews 8:1:

Psalm 113:5–6

1. In Philippians 1:23, being "with Christ" seems to be compared with not being with Him physically. And if it is "far better" to be with Him, what does that tell us about the reality of heaven?

[21] For to me, to live is Christ, and to die is gain. [22] But if I live on in the flesh, this will mean fruit from my labor; yet what I shall choose I cannot tell. [23] For I am hard-pressed between the two, having a desire to depart and be with Christ, which is far better.

[6] So we are always confident, knowing that while we are at home in the body we are absent from the Lord. [7] For we walk by faith, not by sight. [8] We are confident, yes, well pleased rather to be absent from the body and to be present with the Lord.

2. While we are on earth, we have the presence of God with us through the Holy Spirit, yet Paul says in 2 Corinthians 5:6 that we are "absent from the Lord." How do we deal with what could be seen as a contradiction?

3. Imagine what it will be like to be "present with the Lord," as Paul mentions. What do you think that first glimpse of Jesus in heaven will be like?

Prayer Time ▶

Use the *Our Daily Bread* article on the next page as a guide for a devotional and meditation time relating to heaven.

Reflect

How has this study helped you to picture heaven as God's habitation? What images come to mind when you think of God in His heaven?

If you have departed loved ones who are currently with Jesus in heaven, what do you think they might be doing now?

A Better Place

When my friend Marci's father-in-law passed away, she stopped making his favorite dessert: pineapple salad. One day, her little boy asked why she no longer served it. She replied, "It reminds me of Papa, and it makes me sad; Papa really liked that dessert." Her son replied in a chipper tone, "Not better than heaven!"

That little boy had the right idea. Heaven is a much better place. Remembering this can help ease our sadness when things on earth trigger memories of believing loved ones who have passed away. Our friends and family who have heavenly addresses are much happier there because:

- Heaven is God's home. God's followers will enjoy His presence for all eternity (Revelation 21:3–4).

- Heaven is comfortable in every way. Heaven's residents will never be sick or upset (21:4), hungry or thirsty (7:16).

- Heaven is a beautiful place. A "clear as crystal" river will flow from God's throne (22:1), and God himself will give heaven its light (22:5).

Do things in this world sometimes remind you of believers who have moved on to the next world? If so, it's comforting to think that they are now enjoying heaven— a better place by far.

—*Jennifer Benson Schuldt*

REVELATION 21:3—

God Himself will be with them and be their God.

■ Read today's *Our Daily Bread* at **odb.org**

16

2

The Holy City

am sure many Americans who visit Washington DC are impressed as I was when they view its magnificent structures and monuments. A walk down the Federal Mall, going past the Art Institute and the Smithsonian Institution, the towering Washington Monument, the majestic White House, and standing finally in a moment of reflection at the Lincoln Memorial is a thrilling experience. Americans can be proud, in the right sense of the word, of their nation's capital! It ranks with the great cities of the world—Rome, Paris, Tokyo, or Rome—in beauty and splendor.

Yet, every Christian is a citizen of a heavenly city—a city more dazzling and beautiful than anyone on earth has ever seen. Its streets shimmer with gold, and its jeweled walls and foundations glow in a spectrum of color. We are told that it is free from evil of all kinds, and nothing in it will ever tarnish or decay.

You see, a day is coming when our present solar system will be burned with fire and will be replaced by a new heaven and a new earth. Peter wrote:

But the day of the Lord will come as a thief in the night, in which the heavens will pass away with a great noise, and the elements will melt with fervent heat; both the earth and the works that are in it will be burned up (2 PETER 3:10).

According to this prophecy, our universe will be shattered with a mighty roaring sound. It will burst into flames with such intense heat that even the elements that make up matter will be dissolved. The sun, the moon, the planets, and the distant stars will all be engulfed in flame, but this will not be a tragedy. It will not mean annihilation but transformation.

The Word of God declares that out of the ruins will emerge a glorious new world—our eternal home. The apostle John saw it in a vision, and under the inspiration of the Holy Spirit described the scene:

Now I saw a new heaven and a new earth, for the first heaven and the first earth had passed away. Also there was no more sea. Then I,

John, saw the holy city, New Jerusalem, coming down out of heaven from God, prepared as a bride adorned for her husband (REVELATION 21:1-2).

The New Jerusalem, which John proceeded to describe, will rest upon the great planet that will come into existence. This holy city that comes down will be the capital of the new heaven and new earth. It is called the "New Jerusalem" to distinguish it from the two other Jerusalems mentioned in the Bible—the earthly city still in Palestine today and the "heavenly Jerusalem" of Hebrews 12. (The heavenly Jerusalem and the New Jerusalem are actually the same city, but seen at different stages of redemptive history.)

Let's now consider three aspects of this heavenly city, the eternal home of the redeemed: (1) its present location, (2) its place in the coming millennial reign of Christ, and (3) its external appearance as it comes down to rest upon the great planet of the future.

 # The Location of the Heavenly City

The eternal home of the saints is now in heaven as the capital city, which is implied in the name "the heavenly Jerusalem" (Hebrews 12:22). But this raises a question that has often been asked, "Where is heaven?"

Some think it is located somewhere in the northern skies. For biblical evidence to support their position, they point to Psalm 75, which reads in part:

For exaltation comes neither from the east nor from the west nor from the south (V. 6).

They reason that if "exaltation" does not originate from the east, west, or south, it can come only from the north. Thus they conclude that since God is the One who gives blessing, this verse teaches that His throne is located somewhere in the north. In addition, they point out that the altar sacrifice was the brightness of God's glory coming from the north (Ezekiel 1:4).

These scriptural affirmations may give us a hint to the present location of heaven and its capital city, but we can't be sure that it is in some distant place out in space. It may be much nearer to earth than we think, and we need not be disturbed by statements of unbelievers who say that no astronomers have ever seen evidence of its existence. It is foolish to deny that something exists just because it cannot be seen with the eyes or detected by our present equipment. Every scientifically minded person in our modern age realizes that something may be very real while completely imperceptible to us.

We believe beyond all doubt in the existence of a glorious city called "the heavenly Jerusalem." We are confident that the saints of past ages and our loved ones who died in Christ are there now, and that we will someday join them. The patriarchs looked forward to entering this promised city when they died. Abraham left his homeland, an area of well-established cities, to follow the call of God, though he did not know his earthly destination. Nevertheless he was able to exercise great faith and patience while living as a wanderer

> We believe beyond all doubt in the existence of a glorious city called "the heavenly Jerusalem."

because "he waited for the city which has foundations, whose builder and maker is God" (Hebrews 11:10).

Even though Abraham, Isaac, and Jacob were never able to gain full possession of the Promised Land, they did not despair. They realized that a heavenly city was awaiting them. That's the reason the Bible says that "now they desire a better, that is, a heavenly country. Therefore God is not ashamed to be called their God, for He has prepared a city for them" (11:16).

This heavenly city, planned and built by God, is mentioned again in Hebrews 12.

But you have come to Mount Zion and to the city of the living God, the heavenly Jerusalem, to an innumerable company of angels (HEBREWS 12:22).

I repeat, then, that today the great city of God for which Abraham looked is in heaven, the dwelling place of the souls of all believers in Christ who have died. We do not know exactly where heaven with its capital city is located, but we wait for it with hopeful anticipation.

Its Place in the Millennial Kingdom

What will be the location of the heavenly city during the millennial reign of Christ? Some believe that throughout the coming golden age it will be suspended above the earth as a satellite city. While this theory cannot be proven, there is some evidence to substantiate it.

In the first place, the Scriptures indicate that Christ and His glorified saints will rule the earth during the millennial age. Our Lord is depicted as reigning from Jerusalem accompanied by resurrected believers. This does not mean, of course, that the glorified saints will be subjected to the limitations of earthly life. Their home will be heavenly Jerusalem, but they will serve in certain capacities here. Dr. Alvin J. McClain explained it this way:

"The residence of the saints in heaven while ruling on earth, actually, is much less of a problem than that of a businessman whose office is in a city while his residence is in the suburbs."

A number of Bible scholars believe that during the tribulation period, which comes just before the establishment of the millenial kingdom, the heavenly Jerusalem will become visible to earth dwellers. This would be in perfect keeping with the fact that miracles of power will be on open display. Furthermore, in Revelation 13:6 we may have a hint that the people on earth will be able to see the heavenly Jerusalem. We read:

The place where the Lord and His saints will meet in the air could be the location from which they will share with Christ in His rule over the earth during those 1,000 years.

Then he opened his mouth in blasphemy against God, to blaspheme His name, His tabernacle, and those who dwell in heaven.

The Greek text does not contain the word *and*, which we find in our English version. It should read, "Then he opened his mouth for blasphemies against God, to blaspheme His name and His tabernacle—those who dwell in heaven." Could it be that the sight of this satellite city where the saints dwell triggers this blasphemy?

Another indication that the heavenly Jerusalem will be relatively near the earth is found in Paul's description of the rapture and resurrection at Christ's coming for His own. He told the Thessalonian believers that the meeting place will be "in the air."

The Lord Himself will descend from heaven with a shout, with the voice of an archangel, and with the trumpet of God. And the dead in Christ will rise first. Then we who are alive and remain shall be caught up together with them in the clouds to meet the Lord in the air. And thus we shall always be with the Lord (1 THESSALONIANS 4:16–17).

The place where the Lord and His saints will meet in the air could be the location from which they will share with Christ in His rule over the earth during those 1,000 years. If this is true, and the heavenly Jerusalem is a satellite city suspended above the earth, the resurrected and translated saints would have ready access to earth from their dwelling place above. This would facilitate their ruling with Christ, as promised in the Word of God.

A further implication that during the millennial age the heavenly Jerusalem will be a satellite city is found in John's description, which we read earlier, as he saw it descending from heaven (Revelation 21:2). The language used indicates that this city was already in existence before it made its descent to earth. When we recall that Hebrews 12 depicts the "heavenly Jerusalem" as a home of "the spirits of just men made perfect (v. 23), we have good reason to believe that the eternal home of the resurrected believers will be the same city. We find it logical to think of it in three stages: (1) the heavenly Jerusalem where the spirits of the dead now live, (2) the satellite city from which certain believers commute to earth during the millennial age, and (3) the settled city which will ultimately rest upon "a new earth."

 ## Its General Description

John described graphically the coming of the New Jerusalem to the earth. Remember, our solar system will have been dissolved into one great mass by God's fire of judgment, and the new heavens and new earth will have been built out of its ruins. Then John said:

Now I saw a new heaven and a new earth, for the first heaven and the first earth had passed away. Also there was no more sea. Then I, John, saw the holy city, New Jerusalem, coming down out of heaven from God, prepared as a bride adorned for her husband. And I heard a loud voice from heaven saying, "Behold, the tabernacle of God is with men, and He will dwell with them, and they shall be His people. God Himself will be with them and be their God" (REVELATION 21:1–3).

What a breathtaking sight this must have been! And how awesome the voice that declared the glorious truth that God will forever dwell there with His people! As John looked at the city coming down, he saw it glowing with the glory of God. He observed it resting upon its twelve jeweled foundations and rising skyward, sparkling like a diamond in the sunlight and reflecting its brightness over the whole earth. Then John gave its measurements:

He who talked with me had a gold reed to measure the city, its gates, and its wall. The city is laid out as a square; its length is as great as its breadth. And he measured the city with the reed: twelve thousand furlongs. Its length, breadth, and height are equal

(REVELATION 21:15–16).

The New Jerusalem is depicted as being 1,500 miles long and wide. We also read that "its length, breadth, and height are equal." Many Bible students believe these numbers should be taken symbolically and that the city, cubical in form, resembles the shape of the holy of holies in the tabernacle and the temple. There seems to be no good reason, however, to depart from the literal acceptance of the dimensions of the holy city.

Even if we take the numbers literally, though, we cannot speak with absolute certainty about its height. But if the phrase "length, breadth, and height are equal" means that the city is actually 1,500 miles high as well as wide and long, we still cannot be sure that we should take this as depicting the shape of a perfect cube or of a pyramid going up 1,500 miles. Some scholars believe that the word *equal* in this context means that it will be square, and that in height it will be level.

Whether we accept the city as existing in the form of a cube, a pyramid, or a perfectly level square makes very little difference. In either case the size is most amazing. At the ground level it covers more area than India, and if placed in the United States, it would reach from the tip of Maine to the tip of Florida, and from the shore of the Atlantic Ocean westward to Denver. What a city that will be! It will rise up from the earth on twelve foundations of precious jewels and will glow with perpetual light as it reflects the glory of God and shines out through its jasper walls. What beauty! What immensity! No need for anyone to worry about whether or not there will be room for the redeemed!

Yes, glory—indescribable blessedness—will be the eternal portion of all who trust in Jesus Christ. Believers are now citizens of the heavenly Jerusalem, and someday in glorified bodies they will enter the New Jerusalem. What a great salvation is ours! What a wonderful prospect! What a wonderful hope!

To begin to understand the splendor and majesty of the place God has built for us.

MEMORY VERSE
Revelation 21:1—

"Now I saw a new heaven and a new earth, for the first heaven and the first earth had passed away."

Warming Up

Have you ever thought about how many people will be in heaven and how big it will have to be to accommodate all the believers?

Thinking Through

1. When you read Richard DeHaan's comment "a day is coming when our present solar system will be burned with fire" (page 18) and Peter's words in 2 Peter 3:10, what kind of thoughts come to mind? How difficult is it to envision and even accept this scenario?

2. Have you ever given any thought to question: Where is heaven? After reading Richard's comments in connection to Psalm 75:6 (page 19), what goes through your mind about where heaven is?

3. Given the dimensions provided by John in Revelation 21:15–16 (see page 24), what do you think of the possibilities Richard mentioned about the shape of the New Jerusalem? Do these kinds of details matter to you or not?

Going Further

Refer

Examine the following Scripture passages for details about what heaven will be like:

John 14:2

Revelation 21:22–27

2 Peter 3:13

2 Corinthians 5:1

Hebrews 12:22–24

Digging In   Read   Revelation 21:1–3, 5–6

1. When you read John's description of the new heaven as being "prepared as a bride adorned for her husband" (v. 2) what does he mean? And what does that image indicate about how that new heaven will look?

2. Consider what it means that "the tabernacle of God is with men." What are the implications of that for all of us who will be there?

3. What is the significance of the words, "I am the Alpha and the Omega" as it regards this new heaven and new earth?

¹ Now I saw a new heaven and a new earth, for the first heaven and the first earth had passed away. Also there was no more sea. ² Then I, John, saw the holy city, New Jerusalem, coming down out of heaven from God, prepared as a bride adorned for her husband. ³ And I heard a loud voice from heaven saying, "Behold, the tabernacle of God is with men, and He will dwell with them, and they shall be His people. God Himself will be with them and be their God."

⁵ Then He who sat on the throne said, "Behold, I make all things new." And He said to me, "Write, for these words are true and faithful."

⁶ And He said to me, "It is done! I am the Alpha and the Omega, the Beginning and the End. I will give of the fountain of the water of life freely to him who thirsts.

Prayer Time 》

Use the *Our Daily Bread* article on the next page as a guide for a devotional and meditation time relating to heaven.

Reflect

As you think about what you just learned about the new heaven and the new earth, which elements of this study bring the most comfort and hope to you? What do you look forward to the most as you contemplate heaven?

Thoughts of Heaven

Cartoonists often depict those who have gone to heaven as white-robed, ghostly forms floating among the clouds or sitting on golden stairs playing harps. What a far cry from the picture we find in the Bible!

In 1 Corinthians 15, we read that our resurrection bodies, although not subject to death, will be real and tangible—not mere apparitions. And Revelation 21:1–5 tells us that God will bring about "a new heaven and a new earth." He will bring down "the city of the living God, the heavenly Jerusalem" (Hebrews 12:22), and set it upon the new earth as the "New Jerusalem." It is described as having streets, walls, gates, and even a river and trees (Revelation 22:1–5).

Life in that city will be wonderful, free from all the debilitating effects of sin. There will be no more death, sorrow, mourning, and pain, for God will make "all things new." But best of all, He himself will come to live among us, making possible a new level of intimacy with Him.

It's difficult to envision such an existence, but what an exciting prospect! It is all possible because of what Jesus did when He died for us on the cross. This should motivate us to worship Him, live godly lives, and tell others how they too can be assured of a glorious future.

—*Herb Vander Lugt*

REVELATION
21:3—
Behold, the tabernacle of God is with men, and He will dwell with them, and they shall be His people.

■ Read today's
Our Daily Bread at
odb.org

3

The Home of Beauty

The day is coming when a great explosion will occur and a cleansing fire will sweep across our entire planetary system. This catastrophic event will mark the end of time, the final defeat of Satan, and the ushering in of eternity. After describing the millennium, the apostle John said:

Then I saw a great white throne and Him who sat on it, from whose face the earth and the heaven fled away. And there was found no place for them (REVELATION 20:11).

The apostle Peter also described this day of judgment when he wrote:

The heavens will pass away with a great noise, and the elements will melt with fervent heat; both the earth and the works that are in it will be burned up (2 PETER 3:10).

In this manner the material of our present universe will be purged, purified, and transformed. Out of this all-encompassing conflagration will emerge a new planet that John called "a new heaven and a new earth." The heavenly Jerusalem, where the saints of the ages now dwell with Christ will then descend from a region untouched by the flame and come to rest on the new earth, where it will remain forever as the capital city of heaven. It will then be called the New Jerusalem. The apostle John described this great event in Revelation 21.

> Some questions naturally arise: What kind of place will our eternal home be? What will we do there?

When we think about the eternal home of all who believe in Jesus as personal Savior, some questions naturally arise: "What kind of place will it be?" "What will we do there?" Many of our questions are answered in Revelation 21 and 22. Included is a description of the beauty of the heavenly city from without and its glory within. In this chapter we will consider these two aspects of our eternal home.

Its Beauty From Without

Let's imagine we're standing on a vast plain with the heavenly city towering over us in resplendent beauty. We see a brilliant, shining city, with light streaming through its jasper walls and pearly gates, and a full spectrum of color gleaming from its jeweled foundation.

ITS JASPER WALL

As we gaze in awe on the city, the first thing to attract our attention is its massive

> **"The New Jerusalem will be a place of extravagant beauty and natural wonders. It will be a vast Eden, integrated with the best of human culture, under the reign of Christ."** —RANDY ALCORN, *HEAVEN*

jasper wall. The apostle John described it as follows: "Her light was like a most precious stone, like a jasper stone, clear as crystal. Also she had a great and high wall" (Revelation 21:11–12). In verse 17 John said this wall measures 144 cubits in height (216 feet). Even though we may not be able to identify exactly what kind of jasper this is, we do know that these semi-precious stones are translucent in composition, so that light is able to pass through them. From these jasper walls, therefore, radiate brilliant rays of dazzling color for all to see. The glory of the city will thus be visible from afar, and even the dwellers in the area outside the walls will share in its brilliance.

Although the wall around the city is real, it is also symbolic. The purpose of the wall is not to preserve the city against invaders, for God will have no enemies in the new earth. Because it stands 216 feet high, it impressively signifies that no one will enter the city apart from God's grace. The wall is too high to be scaled by human effort, and the only portals are the twelve guarded gates. The requirement for admittance is salvation, and no one who has rejected God's plan will be able to go in. Salvation is the gift of God's grace to those who humbly acknowledge their need of forgiveness and who receive Jesus Christ as Savior.

ITS JEWELED FOUNDATIONS

The next thing to catch our vision as we look at the city is its jeweled foundation. Normally, foundations undergird the walls of a city and lie below the ground where they cannot be seen. But this is not the case in the New Jerusalem, for the foundation supporting its walls is fully visible to all and is indescribably beautiful. Comprising twelve layers of different precious stones—from sapphire to emerald—the wall stretches all the way around the city.

Many Bible scholars believe that these jewels reflect all the colors of the rainbow, although we do not know the precise characteristics of each stone. Beginning at ground level, these were probably the colors seen by the apostle: the **jasper** stone may have been a light green or yellow; the **sapphire**, a sky-blue or azure; the **chalcedony**, containing a combination of colors, was mostly green and blue; the **emerald**, bright green; the **sardonyx**, red and white; the **sardius**, reddish in color; **chrysolite**, golden yellow; **beryl**, sea-green; **topaz**, yellow-green and transparent; **chrysoprasus**, golden-green; **jacinth**, violet; and **amethyst**, either rose-red or purple. The radiating light of the city, shining out through the jasper wall and blazing through the open gates, reflects from those precious stones in splendorous color.

> The gates of heaven are open at all times and in every direction, for salvation is still offered freely to everyone.

The beauty of the city to the observer from the outside will be magnificent, as described in Revelation 21:19–20. In the foundation stones will be inscribed the names of the twelve apostles of the Lamb (v. 14), those valiant men of Israel who first proclaimed the message of a risen Christ to the world.

ITS PEARLY GATES

In the walls of the heavenly city are twelve gates of pearl, and they will never close. Here's John's description:

Also she had a great and high wall with twelve gates, and twelve angels at the gates, and names written on them, which are the names of the twelve tribes of the children of Israel . . . . The twelve gates were twelve pearls; each individual gate was of one pearl. And the street of the city was pure gold, like transparent glass (REVELATION 21:12, 21).

Some Bible scholars believe that these gates of pearl suggest salvation by grace. Even as a wound of an oyster results in the formation of a valuable pearl, the gates of heaven can be entered only because the Lord Jesus was "wounded for our transgressions" (Isaiah 53:5). Although men wickedly rejected Him and crucified Him, it was through this death that salvation was made possible. Now all who believe on Him can look forward to entering the pearly gates of heaven. Jesus himself said, "I am the door. If anyone enters by Me, he will be saved" (John 10:9).

The gates are open at all times and in every direction, for salvation is still offered freely to everyone. The angels who keep watch at the open gates, therefore, are a wonderful contrast to the cherubim who guarded the closed gate of Eden after Adam and Eve sinned. These angels keep the way of access open, while the cherubim kept the Garden closed to fallen humanity.

In the gates are inscribed the names of the twelve tribes of Israel, for "salvation is of the Jews" (John 4:22). The Lord Jesus Christ was born of the seed of Abraham and David, and only those who come through the blessedness of His "Messianic gate" can pass through the pearly gates into heaven.

Its Beauty Within

Having envisioned the beauty of the New Jerusalem from the outside, let us now pass through one of those pearly gates and enter the city. As we cross the threshold, we gaze in wonder, for before us lie a golden street, a crystal river, and the tree of life.

ITS GOLDEN STREET

One of the characteristics of the heavenly city is the abundance of gold. A precious commodity throughout man's history, gold has been used as an overlay in works of art and as a standard of value, and has been the means of both good and evil in society. It served the purposes of God in the tabernacle and temple, for much gold was in evidence there; it was also used by idolators in the making of images. On earth, men have fought, suffered, and died for it. But in the New Jerusalem, gold will be so plentiful that it will be used for paving bricks and building blocks. And it will be like glass, possessing transparent qualities, so that the glorious light of the holy city will both shine through it and be reflected by it. Here is John's description:

The city was pure gold, like clear glass. . . . and the street of the city was pure gold, like transparent glass (REVELATION 21:18, 21).

Traditionally, gold has symbolized purity. In the wedding band, for example, the circle speaks of endlessness and the gold stands for purity. The golden street of the New Jerusalem, therefore, might well suggest the pure and holy walk of God's redeemed in their eternal home. And the brightness of the city, reflecting from the gold that abounds everywhere, will have its uncorrupted counterpart within the heart of every citizen of heaven. Yes, holiness and purity will pervade the eternal city.

ITS CRYSTAL RIVER

A river clear as crystal will flow through the New Jerusalem. The apostle John declared:

He showed me a pure river of water of life, clear as crystal, proceeding from the throne of God and of the Lamb (REVELATION 22:1).

Just as in Eden there was a river to water the garden, so also in the New Jerusalem there will be a river of life. It will begin at the throne of God, the very uppermost part of the city, and it will course downward through the entire area.

Cities have always been dependent on a good water supply, providing for their inhabitants freshness, cleanness, and life. Even today the river continues to be an emblem of fruitfulness, vitality, and abundance, its waters being fed by melting snows and mountain ranges and refreshing springs, and constantly purified as they tumble downward to be used by people. In fact, our Savior very fittingly used the words "rivers of living water" (John 7:38) to indicate the outflow of blessings from the life of the believer through the work of the Holy Spirit.

In the New Jerusalem, a river of crystal will flow forever, reminding us for all eternity that God had graciously and abundantly provided for our every spiritual need.

Remember, life in eternity will not be a nebulous existence in some nameless place. No indeed! We will lead rich and full lives in glorified bodies. We'll dwell on a renewed earth in a real city of gold, and our lives will be filled with significance and meaning as we give praise to our Redeemer and gladly do His bidding.

> Life in eternity will not be a nebulous existence in some nameless place. We will lead rich and full lives in glorified bodies.

This crystal river flowing through our eternal home will be of sparkling beauty and of clarity beyond the purest water man has ever seen. Think of it! All who believe in Christ will walk the banks of this glorious crystal river. What a blessed joy will be ours!

ITS TREE OF LIFE

A third item of special interest in the New Jerusalem will be the tree of life. When Adam and Eve sinned, the Lord God drove them from the Garden of Eden. One reason He did this was to prevent them from having further access to the tree of life. You see, they had rebelled, bringing the curse of death on themselves. The tree of life was therefore out of bounds for them. But in our eternal home we will be free to partake of the fruit of this tree, for Revelation 22 says,

In the middle of its street, and on either side of the river, was the tree of life (v. 2).

The term *tree of life* does not refer to one single tree, but to a species. Apparently there will be many such trees, for we are told that "on either side of the river, was the tree of life." While only one tree of life stood in Eden's garden, here in the New Jerusalem—man's eternal paradise—a multitude of these

> **"Along the bank of the river, on this side and that, will grow all kinds of trees used for food; their leaves will not wither, and their fruit will not fail. They will bear fruit every month, because their water flows from the sanctuary. Their fruit will be for food, and their leaves for medicine."** EZEKIEL 47:12

trees are seen lining the river and producing fruit continuously. Their leaves will be a special blessing to mankind, for John said that "the leaves of the tree were for the healing of the nations" (v. 2).

It's difficult to envision just how the trees, the crystal river, and the street of gold will be related. Some excellent Bible teachers feel that a river will flow through the middle of a broad street, and that alongside the river on each bank will be the trees. Others believe that a grove of trees is centered between the avenue of gold on one side and the river on the other. Regardless of which view you may choose, it's evident that those who conceive of heaven as a place where the redeemed will do nothing but sit on golden stairs playing harps are grossly mistaken. Life in heaven will be filled with beauty and variety.

We've been concerned in this study with what the Bible tells us about our eternal home. We have seen its beauty from without; its gleaming jasper walls, its jeweled foundations, and its gates of pearl. We have also seen its glory within as we have envisioned the street of gold, the crystal river, and the tree of life.

This glimpse of our eternal home should bring two responses to the heart of the true believer in Christ. First, there should be a renewed determination to place top priority on the spiritual and eternal rather than on the physical and temporal. May we therefore, in anticipation of the glory and beauty of our eternal home, begin right now to "lay up . . . treasures in heaven" (Matthew 6:20) by putting the Lord first and by a constant willingness to serve Him.

Second, the thought of heaven should cheer us when we become discontented with life and discouraged about the future. No matter how badly things may be going or how difficult the struggles, the prospect of that wonderful abode awaiting us should be a source of encouragement and hope.

Remember, in heaven we will live forever in the presence of our loving Savior. Life will be rich and full, and we will know a purity, bliss, and love such as could never be experienced here.

The Home of Beauty

STUDY GUIDE

read pages 29–37

3

To see the majesty and glory and unequaled beauty of the New Jerusalem.

MEMORY VERSE
Revelation 21:10—
"He carried me away in the Spirit to a mountain great and high, and showed me the Holy City, Jerusalem, coming down out of heaven from God" (NIV).

Warming Up

Perhaps you've seen some of the great manmade wonders of the world: the Taj Mahal, the Great Wall of China, or Petra. Now consider that heaven will put anything manmade to shame by comparison. Talk about what you know about heaven and how stupendous it will be compared to what mankind has built.

Thinking Through

1. Richard DeHaan's description of the arrival of the new heaven and new earth describes a truly spectacular event. What goes through your mind as you imagine, as he suggests, "standing on a vast plain with the heavenly city towering above" (see page 30)?

2. How familiar are you with jasper, sapphire, emerald, sardonyx, and the other jewels that will make up the city walls? Is there anything you've ever seen that can help you imagine what this will look like?

3. How does the fact that the city will have golden streets symbolize purity and holiness?

Going Further

Refer

Think about how the following verses buttress the idea that what God has prepared in heaven is nearly beyond our description or ability to imagine it.

1 Corinthians 2:9

Revelation 4:1–11

Hebrews 12:22–24

Acts 7:49

1. We don't know what John saw that would have led him to conclude that he was seeing Jerusalem. What might have been some indicators that this was the holy city?

2. What does it tell us about God's great plan for history that the names of the twelve tribes of Israel will be written on the gates (21:12)?

3. What do you think it means to have leaves that are for "the healing of the nations" (22:2)?

[10] And he carried me away in the Spirit to a great and high mountain, and showed me the great city, the holy Jerusalem, descending out of heaven from God, [11] having the glory of God. Her light was like a most precious stone, like a jasper stone, clear as crystal. [12] Also she had a great and high wall with twelve gates, and twelve angels at the gates, and names written on them, which are the names of the twelve tribes of the children of Israel.

[1] And he showed me a pure river of water of life, clear as crystal, proceeding from the throne of God and of the Lamb. [2] In the middle of its street, and on either side of the river, was the tree of life, which bore twelve fruits, each tree yielding its fruit every month. The leaves of the tree were for the healing of the nations. [3] And there shall be no more curse, but the throne of God and of the Lamb shall be in it, ... [6] Then he said to me, "These words are faithful and true." And the Lord God of the holy prophets sent His angel to show His servants the things which must shortly take place.

Prayer Time »

Use the *Our Daily Bread* article on the next page as a guide for a devotional and meditation time relating to heaven.

Reflect

Of all the traits that you've read about concerning heaven in this study, which seem to you to be the most beautiful?

What Will We Do?

'm sometimes asked what we'll do in heaven. Will we sit on clouds and strum celestial harps? Will we flit about on gossamer wings? In his vision, John the apostle saw three future heavenly activities.

1. The first one is serving (Revelation 22:3). Perhaps we'll explore an unknown corner of the universe, or, as C. S. Lewis suggests, govern a distant star. Whatever that service may entail, there will be no sense of inadequacy, no weakness, no weariness. In heaven we'll have minds and bodies equal to the task to which we're assigned.

2. The second activity is seeing. We "shall see His face" (v. 4). "Now we see in a mirror, dimly" (1 Corinthians 13:12), but in heaven we shall see our Savior face to face, and we "shall be like Him" (1 John 3:2). This is what Revelation 22:4 means when it says, "His name shall be on their foreheads." The name of God represents His perfect character, so to bear His name means to be like Him. In heaven we will never again struggle with sin but will reflect the beauty of His holiness forever.

3. Finally, there is reigning. We shall serve our King by ruling and reigning with Him "forever and ever" (v. 5).

What will we do in heaven? We'll serve God, see our Savior, and reign with Him forever. We'll be busy!

—*David Roper*

REVELATION 22:3–4—

His servants shall serve Him. They shall see His face, and His name shall be on their foreheads.

■ Read today's *Our Daily Bread* at **odb.org**

4

The Home of Blessedness

The pain, sorrow, and unhappiness in this world of ours are distressing to any sensitive individual. Starvation is rampant in some parts of the globe, mothers and their children have been left homeless by war, and young and old alike are destroying their lives inch by inch through alcohol and drug abuse. Crime continues to threaten security and safety for many. Selfishness and sin have turned our earthly home into a habitat of untold suffering and wickedness.

A time is coming, however, when all of this will be changed. Our solar system will be purged by a great consuming fire, and it will be replaced by a new heaven and a new earth. Writing in Revelation 21 and 22, the apostle John recorded his vision of an immense city of shimmering beauty, descending slowly from heaven to become the capital city of our eternal home. It will be radiant with the light of God's glory shining through jasper walls, its jeweled foundation, and its pearly gates. And this city, the new Jerusalem, will be the eternal abode of all who have placed their faith in Jesus Christ. All who have been saved will walk the streets of gold in transformed, glorified bodies. We'll enjoy heaven's beautiful crystal river and have ready access to the tree of life. We'll be eternally delivered from every evil and burden that plagues our world today. And we'll finally have become what God intended us to be.

What a wonderful life we'll have in our eternal home! In that perfect society we'll realize our full spiritual potential as individuals. Having entered an eternal fellowship with God, we'll be engaged in an endless variety of meaningful activities. We'll join with the saints of all ages in a spirit of communion, fellowship, and love—all centered on the Lord Jesus Christ.

In this concluding lesson on heaven, I'd like to consider with you some of the marvelous blessings that await us. We'll see that the imperfections of this life will be missing and that positive blessings will be there in abundance.

 # The Effects of Sin Removed

So that we may more completely understand the blessings and glory of our life in heaven, John's record mentions a number of things that mar human existence on earth, and it assures us that they will not be present in our eternal home.

NO TEARS

Our days on earth are filled with tragedy, suffering, disappointment, and evil. As a result, tears are all too common in the experience of mankind. The lonely vigils at bedsides, the secret burdens buried deep in a mother's heart, and the memories of tragedy, rejection, and pain are all too close to us. But before eternity begins, God himself will wipe away all tears from our eyes! The ministry will not be entrusted to angels. No lesser citizens of heaven will perform this task, for the Lord himself will pour His healing balm into the wounds and hurts of our lives. The apostle John wrote:

God will wipe away every tear from their eyes; there shall be no more death, nor sorrow, nor crying. There shall be no more pain, for the former things have passed away (REVELATION 21:4).

Let me be quick to point out that these words in no way imply that saints will shed tears in heaven concerning the sins and failures of their earthly lives. Not at all! The gracious, comforting work of God, not the remorse of His children, is the emphasis of this verse.

NO DEATH

Not only will there be an absence of tears of sadness in heaven, but John also said, "There shall be no more death" (Revelation 21:4). This fearsome enemy continually casts its shadow on our lives here on earth. Eventually death enters every happy family circle. Sooner or later, every home experiences the feeling of emptiness—the dreadful vacuum caused by the passing of a loved one. No member of humanity, even the most strong, can escape the relentless passing of time and the realization that the earthly sojourn is brief. How happy we can be that in our eternal home we will experience no more anxiety, no more

Are you burdened today with some seemingly insurmountable problem? Are you lonely, heartbroken and disappointed? Have the tears flowed freely throughout the dark and long hours of the night? Then, if you are a child of God, dwell upon this happy thought: the day is coming when "sorrow and sighing" shall be no more—"only glory by and by!" With that prospect you can say with Paul, "...the sufferings of this present time are not worthy to be compared with the glory which shall be revealed in us" (ROMANS 8:18). A brighter day is coming when words such as *sighing, death,* and *tears* will all be obsolete. So, don't be downhearted, beloved; keep looking up !

—RICHARD W. DEHAAN, *OUR DAILY BREAD*

wondering when the end will come, no more long hours by hospital bedsides, and praise God, no more funerals!

NO SORROW NOR CRYING

These words are closely related to the tears God wipes away, but the sorrow from our eternal home has reference to mourning or grief. Here on earth we have many occasions for sorrow—our own sins and shortcomings, personal misfortunes, disappointments in others, and distressing national conditions. When we reach the New Jerusalem, we shall never again mourn, but we'll be completely free from sin, experience no adversity or discouragement, and never have occasion to be concerned over calamitous national or world conditions. In James 4:9 sinners are warned to change their laughter into mourning, but in heaven the saints will exchange mourning for joy.

We also are reassured that there will be no more crying. This refers to loud, uncontrolled sobbing—the kind of weeping that results from the shock of deep, piercing hurt. Thank God, when we reach the eternal home, we will never again hear agonizing cries of sorrow or anguish. There will be no heartbreak in heaven.

NO PAIN

We are also given the comforting assurance that "there shall be no more pain" (Revelation 21:4). What a blessing to read those words from the Bible! A brief visit to a cancer ward, convalescent home, or hospital quickly gives us an unforgettable glimpse of the widespread suffering that curses our world. In heaven, however, we will never again experience hurt of any kind. These bodies of ours in their glorified state will be free from all disease. We'll never again know physical distress or suffering. And we'll never grow old. A feeling of vigor and youthful energy will forever mark the resurrection body that will be ours.

NO NIGHT

We are also told that night will never fall in heaven. "The city had no need of the sun or of the moon to shine in it, for the glory of God illuminated it. The Lamb is its light. And the nations of those who are saved shall walk in its light, and the kings of earth bring their glory and honor into it. Its gates shall not be shut at all by day (there shall be no night there)" (Revelation 21:23–25).

In the present, we're dependent on the sun for light and heat. We have day and night, and the four seasons, because of the earth's rotation and our relationship to the sun. In heaven, however, there will be no need of sunlight, for the radiant glory of God will fill the city and spread throughout the entire earth.

NO DEFILEMENT

Another element common to this life that will be missing in heaven will be defilement from evil. Revelation 21:27 tells us that "there shall by no means enter it anything that defiles, or causes an abomination or a lie." Today our larger society is marked by crime, violence, obsenity, and hatred. Pornography, obscene theatrical productions, and blatant immorality pervade our world. In many areas, parents can no longer allow their children to walk to the playground alone, for fear they will be harmed. Drug addiction and its related evils and heartaches threaten people from all walks of life. Violent crimes such as rape, armed robbery, and murder continue to cast fear among citizens.

The promise of no defilement in heaven, therefore, comes as good news. Within the gates of the New Jerusalem no sin can enter. No defiling substance nor personal acts of desecration can mar its eternal purity. And no spiritual or physical harm will ever come to any of God's children.

Think of it! No rebellion! No murder! No violence! No immorality! What a blessed place heaven will be!

NO CURSE

Another effect of sin that will be removed forever when we enter our eternal home is found in the promise that "there shall be no more curse" (Revelation 22:3). In our world, farmers must toil endlessly in their battle against weeds, poor soil, plant disease, and insects. A violent storm can wipe out a year's crops in a few minutes. But in heaven, nothing will impair productivity. All the effects of Adam's curse will be gone forever. Fields and orchards will flourish. Finally delivered from the consequences of Adam's fall, nature will smile on mankind. We'll experience an abundance that has been unknown since the fall of man.

In our eternal home, we will be free from tears, death, sorrow, crying, pain, darkness, and disappointment. How comforting and strengthening it is to reflect on the curse-free world that awaits us! The tears and sorrows of this life will only serve to make heaven all the sweeter.

Man's Destiny Fulfilled

The evils that mar our life on earth will be gone in heaven, and we will fulfill perfectly the purpose for which God created us: to enjoy His presence, fellowship, and blessing. God has planned that we should be exalted above angels, for they are "sent forth to minister for those who will inherit salvation" (Hebrews 1:14).

WE WILL KNOW HIM PERFECTLY

Our present knowledge of God, while real and precious, remains incomplete. Sin has entered and distorted the picture, and we often fall short of the Lord's ideal for us. But in heaven we will know Him perfectly. We'll behold the glory of His presence, and faith will turn to sight.

I heard a loud voice from heaven saying, "Behold, the tabernacle of God is with men, and He will dwell with them, and they shall be His people. God Himself will be with them and be their God" (REVELATION 21:3).

Yes, we will delight in the glory of the Lord God. And we will know Him personally, for the Bible says:

They shall see His face, and His name shall be on their foreheads (REVELATION 22:4).

Our hearts will throb with joy as we comprehend the fullness of the Lord's glory and majesty. Loving adoration and sincere praise will flow from our hearts as we gaze into the face of our Savior.

WE WILL WORSHIP AND SERVE HIM

In addition to the blessing of knowing and enjoying God, we will be kept busy in fruitful activity.

There shall be no more curse, but the throne of God and of the Lamb shall be in it, and His servants shall serve Him (REVELATION 22:3).

Sometimes heaven is incorrectly pictured as a place of never-ending boredom and sameness. Its inhabitants are portrayed as floating around on clouds, wearing long white robes, and playing harps all day. Or they are depicted as standing forever around the throne of God, mouthing His praises in unison for all eternity.

I'm glad that's not the accurate story. We'll worship God! It will be an important and rewarding part of our heavenly activity. The shortcomings and

■ FOCAL POINT

"Certainly those who live and reign with Christ forever will find the diversity and complexity of their worship of God not less, but richer, in the life to come. Every legitimate activity of new creaturely life will be included within the life of worship of God's people."

—CORNELIUS VENEMA, *THE PROMISE OF THE FUTURE*

imperfections of our praise here will all be removed. Our minds won't wander during prayer as they do now, and we won't be thinking about business or other less important matters when our full attention should be directed toward God.

No temple will be needed in the New Jerusalem (Revelation 21:22), for it would be an element of the imperfect, symbolic worship of this world.

The new world will also present opportunity for an endless variety of activities. The joys we derive from God's beautiful world of nature will still be ours, only on a far higher plane. The delight of fellowship with others will also exceed anything we have ever experienced on earth. In our heavenly home we will know one another perfectly, and each will be without fault.

Our fellowship today is often marred by evasion and a covering of our deepest thoughts, but then a wonderful spirit-to-spirit communion of radiant personalities will exist. Remember, the verse said, "His servants shall serve Him." We'll be busy doing things He considers important, and we'll be infinitely happy as we do His will. Yes, in our eternal home we'll know a life of praise, satisfaction, and usefulness such as we have never experienced here on earth.

WE WILL REIGN WITH HIM

Finally, all believers in Christ will reign with the Lord Jesus for all eternity. The apostle John, after describing the light of God's glory that will surround us, revealed that we will share in His dominion over the earth. He declared:

There shall be no night there: They need no lamp nor light of the sun, for the Lord God gives them light. And they shall reign forever and ever (REVELATION 22:5)**.**

    This completes our glorification. We will actually share in the authority of God over the transformed creation. Exalted far above the angels, transformed into the likeness of Jesus Christ, set free from all pain, sadness, sin, and death, we'll enjoy a life of never-ending happiness, satisfaction, and glory. We will have realized the purpose for which God made us, for with Jesus Christ we will exercise dominion over the earth.

4 The Home of Blessedness

STUDY GUIDE

read pages 41–49

To anticipate the unspeakable blessings that we will enjoy in heaven.

MEMORY VERSE
Revelation 21:4—

"God will wipe away every tear from their eyes; there shall be no more death, nor sorrow, nor crying. There shall be no more pain, for the former things have passed away."

Warming Up

Think about the no mores: death, sorrow, crying, pain. Which of these sounds the most marvelous to you as you think about an eternal life devoid of these things?

Thinking Through

1. Richard DeHaan says, "In that perfect society we'll realize our full spiritual potential" (see page 42). As you think of what that means to you, what spiritual trait do you want to see perfected in your life?

2. Revelation 21:4 says, "God will wipe away every tear from their eyes." But sometimes, we cry tears of joy. Does this verse suggest we will be emotionless, or will we just respond differently in heaven to avoid any kind of tears?

3. The elimination of defilement in heaven—plus the consideration of our continual joy—leads to this thought: On earth, people find much of their joy in sin and even think you cannot have "fun" without sin. What does the truth about no defilement and boundless joy teach us about living in the here and now?

Going Further

Refer

What blessings of heaven are mentioned in the following verses?

2 Peter 3:13

Matthew 25:46

Revelation 11:19

Revelation 2:7

Revelation 7:9

1. Think for a moment what verse 3 is saying. What ideas go through your mind as you contemplate God and man dwelling together?

³ And I heard a loud voice from heaven saying, "Behold, the tabernacle of God is with men, and He will dwell with them, and they shall be His people. God Himself will be with them and be their God. ⁴ And God will wipe away every tear from their eyes; there shall be no more death, nor sorrow, nor crying. There shall be no more pain, for the former things have passed away."
⁷ He who overcomes shall inherit all things, and I will be his God and he shall be My son.

2. Imagine what the beginning of verse 4 means. Imagine standing before the God of the universe as He does this for you. Do you think this means a physical wiping away? Will He offer solace for all the tears of your lifetime? What do you think will be the reality behind this word picture?

3. Verse 7 talks about an inheritance. What do you think it means that you could "inherit all things"?

Prayer Time

Use the *Our Daily Bread* article on the next page as a guide for a devotional and meditation time relating to heaven.

Reflect

Pain and sorrow are so prevalent in this life. What life struggles are you looking forward to seeing removed forever in heaven?

Do you enjoy worship? Imagine how much greater our worship will be when we are face to face with the object of our worship. What does this mean to you?

A Forever Hello

After a week's vacation with her daughter and 4-month-old grandson, Oliver, Kathy had to say goodbye until she could see them again. She wrote to me saying, "Sweet reunions like we had make my heart long for heaven. There, we won't have to try to capture memories in our mind. There, we won't have to pray for the time to go slowly and the days to last long. There, our hello will never turn into goodbye. Heaven will be a 'forever hello,' and I can't wait." As a first-time grandma, she wants to be with her grandson Oliver as much as possible! She's thankful for any time she can be with him and for the hope of heaven—where the wonderful moments will never end.

Our good days do seem too short, and our difficult days far too long. But both kinds of days cause us to long for even better days ahead. The apostle Paul said that he and the Corinthians longed to be "clothed instead with our heavenly dwelling, so that what is mortal may be swallowed up by life" (2 Corinthians 5:4 NIV). Although the Lord is with us in this life, we cannot see Him face to face. Now we live by faith, not by sight (v. 7).

God made us for the very purpose of being near to Him always (v. 5). Heaven will be a forever hello.

—*Anne Cetas*

2 CORINTHIANS 5:5—

He who has prepared us for this very thing is God, who also has given us the Spirit.

■ Read today's *Our Daily Bread* at **odb.org**

5

Racing
To
Heaven

[Note: The following was written by Dave Branon, editor of the DSBS series]

The author of this study, Richard W. DeHaan, died in 2002. When he left us that year at the age of 79, he immediately encountered the realities he had so carefully researched and written about for this booklet. Richard had enjoyed a long lifetime of service for His Savior through RBC Ministries as a teacher and writer, and as the organization's president for many years. And at his death Richard escaped the pain of his Parkinson's disease, the infirmity of his failing heart, and the irritation of his ongoing eye problems. With life's difficulties then behind him, Richard—because of his faith in Jesus Christ—awoke to the heavenly blessing of being "absent from the body and . . . present with the Lord" (2 Corinthians 5:6–8).

For the DeHaan family, and for all of us who have lost Christ-following loved ones to death, the knowledge that they transitioned to a life of transformation and renewal in God's presence gives us hope, blessing, and encouragement.

Richard has clearly spelled out for us in these pages a future that he was an-

---

● FOCAL POINT

"[In 2 Corinthians 5:8, Paul is saying, 'heaven is a better place.' The Word of God says so, and we believe it. And because it's a better place, we'd rather be there. And what makes it a better place is it is at home with the Lord. . . . Paul says we prefer to be absent from the body. If you want to know what I want, I'd like to be out of this body and get there where I belong."

—JOHN MACARTHUR, *FACING DEATH CONFIDENTLY*

---

ticipating as he wrote about it in the prime of his life and that he is now enjoying to its fullest. He wrote glowingly of the **hope** of each follower of Jesus—knowing that although this earth is a grand and glorious place to live, being in God's home for all eternity "is far better" (Philippians 1:23).

He wrote with anticipation of the **blessings** that lie ahead for the believer in heaven: the joy of being in God's presence and the surety of knowing that he or she "will never die" (John 11:26).

And he wrote of the **encouragement** that all of us understand when we have lost a loved one who we know has moved on to a heavenly home that will put them out of reach forever of tears, death, sorrow, pain, and defilement.

Richard, even while writing this booklet, was heading for heaven.

Can I tell you a little story about two young girls who were also on their way to heaven—but who didn't have to wait until they were 79 years old to get there?

Racing To Heaven

This is about two teenagers—my daughter Melissa (who died just a little more than a month before Richard's death) and Emily—two girls who are in that great place of hope, blessing, and encouragement today. As you think about your life and where it is heading, please consider the ultimate destination of these two beautiful teens.

The painting is called *The Homecoming*, and it was created by an artist who lives not far from our hometown. Just before Christmas one year, a friend gave me a print of that painting to take to my wife and told me about the little shop where she bought it.

I took the print home to Sue, and she fell in love with the painting, which depicts the artist's idea of what heaven could be like as loved ones who are already on the other side await the arrival of new residents of the celestial city. Sue was so

enamored with the print that she asked me to go to the nearby town the next day to purchase a few of them for her friends who had also, as we had done, seen a beloved child ushered into glory.

When I arrived at the small-town gallery, I got a bonus. In addition to meeting the artist, I met Selena, a woman with whom I had corresponded by e-mail. Selena and her husband, just like Sue and I, had lost their seventeen-year-old volleyball-loving daughter in a car accident. In addition to meeting the mom, I discovered something special about the painting my wife liked so much.

The artist had used Emily, Selena's daughter, as a reference, so Em was in the painting. And in the painting, this beautiful young teen was racing toward heaven, depicted as a city.

Those of us who have lost teenagers remember with fondness how they lived their lives, full of excitement and boundless energy. Emily and Melissa were always on the run—always going from one sports event to the next school event to the next church activity—barely stopping at home to let the car cool down while they scheduled their next adventure.

Who knew that in their rush they were running for heaven?

Who knew that in their hurry to live life with vigor, they were actually cramming as much in as possible because seventeen years isn't enough time to do everything a teen wants to accomplish?

Fortunately, Emily and Melissa were running toward heaven. Each had a solid faith in Jesus Christ, meaning that when their lives ended too prematurely for us, they were ready to step on shore and see Jesus welcoming them face to face.

The Homecoming is just a painting. But it is a reminder of the importance of making sure that no matter how hectic and active our lives are, the one thing that has to be true is that we are running toward heaven—that we have settled the sin problem by trusting Jesus and that our last breath on earth will be followed by our first breath in heaven.

Racing toward heaven. That's the direction Emily and Melissa were taking. That's the direction we all need to be taking.

—FROM *BEYOND THE VALLEY* BY DAVE BRANON,
DISCOVERY HOUSE PUBLISHERS

At the end of Richard DeHaan's original version of this booklet, he penned the following invitation:

"You can make certain right now that heaven will be your eternal home by praying something like this:

'Lord Jesus, I want heaven to be my home. Therefore, believing that you died for me and arose from the grave, I accept you and the salvation you have provided. Forgive my sin. I'm trusting you and you alone for my salvation. Save me. I do believe. Amen.' "

Remember that Jesus said, "The one who comes to Me I will by no means cast out" (John 6:37). What a joy it is to trust Jesus as Savior, to realize that our sins have been forgiven, and to know that someday—like Richard, Emily, and Melissa—we can run to heaven, to that grand, glorious, and eternal place of hope, blessing, and encouragement!

Are you ready to go?

5 Racing to Heaven

MEMORY VERSE
Hebrews 11:10—

"For he was looking forward to the city with foundations, whose architect and builder is God" (NIV).

To make sure that you are on your way to God's great place of hope, blessing, and encouragement.

Warming Up

Have you ever thought of what it will be like when that great reunion happens in heaven? When you will finally be face to face with your loved ones who have gone before— and with Jesus?

Thinking Through

1. Richard DeHaan had spent countless hours studying what God's Word says about heaven, and that study gave him much hope and courage for the future. What are three things you learned in Richard's study that can help you as you look ahead?

2. Have you, like Melissa's and Emily's families, lost someone in the prime of life? How does Richard's study and even the idea of *The Homecoming* give you help and encouragement as you think of the one you lost?

3. Are you absolutely sure that you have put your faith in Jesus Christ—which opens the door to heaven for you? If you have any doubts, please read Richard's words on page 57 and discuss this matter with someone who you know is a believer.

Going Further

Refer

Compare what these verses tell us about heaven:

John 14:2

Luke 23:43

John 3:16

2 Corinthians 5:1

1. Think about the contrast between the "tent" that is our earthly house and the "building from God" (v. 1). Both are God's construction, but what is different and special about the second one? _____

_____

_____

_____

_____

2. The Word of God tells us of the new home prepared for us, and that is truth. But God also gives us a guarantee of our future glory. What is that and why is it so special (v. 5)? _____

_____

_____

_____

_____

3. While we are still on this earth, we long for our future home. Yet we have a job to do while we wait. What is that job, according to verse 9? _____

_____

_____

_____

_____

_____

_____

¹ For we know that if our earthly house, this tent, is destroyed, we have a building from God, a house not made with hands, eternal in the heavens. ² For in this we groan, earnestly desiring to be clothed with our habitation which is from heaven, ³ if indeed, having been clothed, we shall not be found naked. ⁴ For we who are in this tent groan, being burdened, not because we want to be unclothed, but further clothed, that mortality may be swallowed up by life. ⁵ Now He who has prepared us for this very thing is God, who also has given us the Spirit as a guarantee.

⁶ So we are always confident, knowing that while we are at home in the body we are absent from the Lord. ⁷ For we walk by faith, not by sight. ⁸ We are confident, yes, well pleased rather to be absent from the body and to be present with the Lord.

⁹ Therefore we make it our aim, whether present or absent, to be well pleasing to Him.

Prayer Time ⟫

Use the *Our Daily Bread* article on the next page as a guide for a devotional and meditation time relating to heaven.

Reflect

How has Richard's study given you hope, blessing, and encouragement? _____

_____

Is it possible to enjoy life to the fullest while still anticipating being "present with the Lord"? How does that happen for you? _____

_____

_____

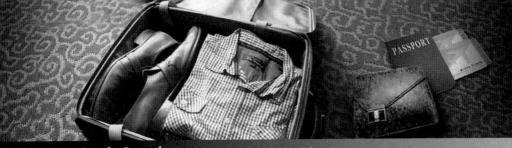

Be Prepared

Just as her friends were doing, my daughter Melissa was busily preparing for adulthood. At school, she was getting ready for college by taking the right courses and had signed up for the ACT college entrance test.

Outside of class, Melissa was learning the socialization skills it takes to get along with people by spending time with friends, classmates, and teammates. At her job, she was learning the relational skills needed for a future career of work. At home, Mell was preparing for future family life by experiencing the way a Christian family would interact.

Getting ready for life as an adult takes work, and Melissa was making good progress.

But none of that preparation was what she would need. In 2002, when she died in a car accident at age 17, the only preparation that mattered was her readiness for heaven.

When the truest test of preparedness came so suddenly on that beautiful June evening—when eternity's door opened for Melissa—she was prepared. She had put her faith in Jesus and trusted His sacrifice on the cross for her sins (John 3:16; Romans 5:8–9).

When she faced the ultimate test of being prepared, Melissa was ready. Are you?

—*Dave Branon*

Romans 5:9—
Having now been justified by His blood, we shall be saved from wrath.

■ Read today's *Our Daily Bread* at **odb.org**

● LEADER'S and USER'S GUIDE

Overview of Lessons: Heaven

Pulpit Sermon Series (for pastors and church leaders)

Although the Discovery Series Bible Study is primarily for personal and group study, pastors may want to use this material as the foundation for a series of messages on this important issue. The suggested topics and their corresponding texts from the Overview of Lessons above can be used as an outline for a sermon series.

DSBS User's Guide (for individuals and small groups)

Individuals—Personal Study

• Read the designated pages of the book.

• Carefully consider the study questions, and write out answers for each.

Small Groups—Bible-Study Discussion

• To maximize the value of the time spent together, each member should do the lesson work prior to the group meeting.

• Recommended discussion time: 45 minutes.

• Engage the group in a discussion of the questions—seeking full participation from each member.

Note To The Reader

The publisher invites you to share your
response to the message of this book
by writing Discovery House Publishers,
P.O. Box 3566, Grand Rapids, MI 49501,
USA. For information about other
Discovery House books, music, videos,
or DVDs, contact us at the same address
or call 1–800–653–8333. Find us on the
Internet at **dhp.org** or send e-mail to
books@dhp.org.